The Barbados I

Grew Up In

A collection of memories by

Graydon Jemmott

"To my good friend DON a man of
substance"

Graydon Jemmott

6/16/21

Preface

At times when I reflect on my life, I ask myself some questions when I see how the communities in Barbados are living today. One of those questions is, if given a choice between my era and now, which one would I choose? I think that I would choose my period; because back then the saying was true, the community did help raise the child. With one caveat, the absence of the beatings I got from my father. This is why I wrote this collection of memories of my era.

With all the advancement we have made, it would be nice if we could go back to that time for a brief moment and show this generation of today how things were. The way communities worked as a unit, the slower pace of life, and the respect for property and person.

I still get a smile on my face when I remember the community back then. People would go away leaving their homes wide open, and not having to worry that someone might enter and steal or do damage to their property. And if the rain came while they were away, a neighbour would go and close up the house for them. Also, as a child back then you had to respect the elders. For example, if your parents and someone in the neighbourhood had a disagreement, and if when you later saw that person you still better say good morning or whatever time of the day it was. If not you would get a good ass whipping for not showing respect.

One - The School Years

The Barbados I grew up in was a nice place in a time that still holds some good and not so good memories for me. It was a time when people cared for each other and looked out for one another.

Back then, the community helped raise the children. As a child growing up in Barbados, you could go from one neighbourhood to the next and didn't have to worry about anything. Everyone knew who you were, so you'd better be on your best behaviour. I am sorry to say that it doesn't happen in today's Barbados society anymore. Everyone looks out for themselves. I was born on July 5,1945, to Louise and Kenrick Jemmott. My parents were hard working people. My father worked for the Government, building and maintaining roads. He also worked part time in a quarry cutting soft stones. My mother worked as a domestic and was also a fish hawker. The Jemmotts were the poorest of the poor in Buccary in those days.

One of my first memories is when I was 3 years old. The neighbourhood kids would play games such as stick and ball, bat and ball and cricket. A lot of the time there would be those of us who were naked, some may have a top on, some may have a bottom on, but at three years old who cares, we only wanted to play. I was one of the naked ones.

When the time came for me to go to school, I was not a happy child. My brother Warren who is three years older took me to school. Going to school meant the loss of our play time. It also meant there was no time for going house to house to get something to eat, which I really enjoyed. The St. John the Baptist Boys School was about two miles away in Holders Hill from-Paynes Bay where we lived. Back then, there was no horse and buggy to take you to school. We had to walk and that was not easy for us, since we went to school barefoot. The route was a tar road and as you can imagine you wouldn't want to be on that road when the sun was shining hot. We would do this walk four times a day because we went home for lunch. I always looked forward to going home when school was dismissed at 3pm.

Going to school was always a challenge for me. Some of the teachers were mean, one in particular was Mr. Haynes. If you didn't behave in his class, he would call you up to the front by the blackboard, take one of the spare pegs that holds up the board and beat you on your forehead with it. I was a victim on many occasions, and it hurt like hell. Back then you didn't tell your parents what the teachers or even the priest said and did to you because they wouldn't believe what you had to say. There were a few good teachers though, like Mr. Roach and Mr. Jones, the headmaster. If you were unlucky enough to be sent to the headmaster, he would flog you with a long leather strap that he kept in his desk. We had a nickname for each teacher, Mr. Jones' nickname was *(Mr. Jones "the crappo stones")*. But of course, we used these names behind their backs, not to their faces.

As I look back, there were some good memories from those years at school. The kids who couldn't keep up with the class would be put into the "Special Class;" when you were in that class you had to go and work in the school's Kitchen Garden. I was one of those kids. Something good came out of that experience for me later in my life, I was able to use what I learned about growing different vegetables and how to work the soil. The kitchen garden was big, and we grew all kinds of vegetables such as, tomatoes, lettuce, carrots, potatoes, cucumbers and on and on. The garden was a source of income for the school. We were free labour for the school.

I finished school at fourteen years old, which added more trouble to my life. My father was also a worker of the land.

Every day after school my brother Warren and I had to go and work with him: Sometimes we pulled weeds. Other times we planted different crops such as corn, sugarcane, or sweet potatoes. I got into trouble often with my dad for not finishing all the work he left for me to do. When he came home and saw what work had not been done, he would give me a whipping. But the beatings didn't make me work any harder.

One time my father tied me to a tree and beat the living shit out of me. I still have the marks on my back from the rope he used to beat me. I was never one to stay at home and I loved to go play with my friends. One friend in particular, Thomas and I, would play all day long, but I always tried to get home before my parents did. If not, I would be in trouble again. My parents came to realize that the flogging I was getting was doing no good, so they came up with an idea they thought would keep me at home. The idea was to put one of my mom's dresses on me to wear at home, thinking that would make me stay. It didn't work. I was not ashamed to wear the dress, of course my friends made fun of me. One said, "that the dress looks better on me than on my Mother." My friends called me "gown-gown", that's one of the nicknames that stuck with me for quite a while.

Two - My Best Friend

What my parents didn't know was that when they left for work, I would go to my friend Thomas' house. I would take off the dress and put on some of his clothes. Then off we'd go to play or do whatever came to mind. Thomas' family liked me, especially his mother and grandmother. His mom, whenever I came around, she would say "Tommy your shadow is here!" We were always inseparable We would go to the beach, play cricket, swim, or go fishing off the rocks. Oftentimes, we would stay on the beach until his grandfather and uncle, along with the other fishermen, came in from the sea to see what the catch of the day would be. Most of the time it would be flying-fish. Other times it could be shark, or dolphin or whatever else they were able to catch. Fishermen are known for their good cooking, so it wasn't unusual that some of us kids would go looking for leftovers from their lunch. That food was so damn sweet.

It was fun going to the beach especially when the fishing boats were on the horizon coming in. There would be a little back and forth as to whose boat it was coming in. One would say, "he knows the boat by the cut of the sails," another would say, "he knows this boat from the draft it is making." The boats didn't come right back to shore, they would anchor about half a mile offshore. If there were any fish, they would be transferred from the boat to a Moses that was tied to their anchor. They would then row Moses to shore. When at shore there were plenty of people to help pull the Moses up onto the beach. This is where the fun began, with so many hawkers looking to buy fish and beat their competitors, sometimes fights would break out.

What we learned was that some fishermen are nicer than others. When the flying-fish were in abundance we would go begging. Some would give you; others would tell you to "f___" off. There's nothing like a good roast flying-fish eaten in the sea, the head and all. Even now in my golden years, I still enjoy a good fish-head. Sometimes sharks would be plentiful, and that was a good thing for us because the fisherman would have to gut the shark before it could be sold. During the gutting process, some men would ask if they could have the sharks' liver. The prized liver is put in a big pot over a fire on the beach, and it was boiled for hours. When the liver was cooked, it would be strained through a brown crocus bag from the boiling pot to another pot, where the oil was collected. The byproduct of the process looks like hamburger meat and is good eating with some salt bread or crispy biscuits. However, you'd better not travel too far from home because that stuff would clean you out.

The Shark oil was then collected and put into a variety of containers ready for sale. When the word got out there was shark liver on the beach, people from all over the neighbourhood would come looking to buy some of the shark liver oil. Parents loved to keep the oil on hand to give to the children when they were not feeling well, and it was good for many ailments. At our house, our mother would make us take a teaspoon of it once a month. Sick or not sick you had to take it on a Friday night or Saturday morning. If we didn't give our mother any trouble (such as crying), she would put some sugar in it for us to take some of the bitterness out of it.

Three – Life in Buccary

At times, I would be late getting back to Thomas' house to change back into the dress. Chances are one of my folks would be home. If my mother was home, I was safe. She would say, "Boy, why are you so hard ears?" But she wouldn't rat me out to my dad. I loved my mom. If my dad was home, I would go and hide at my grandmother's house located in front of ours in Buccary. If or when my dad started looking for me, I would come out as if I had been there the whole time.

Buccary was a little village within a village in Laynes Gap, Paynes Bay in St. James parish. Back in the day, Buccary was a close-knit family community. There were the Morris', the Chandlers, the Grants, my family the Jemmotts, and my grandmother Miss Batson. Most of the houses had a backyard and land for growing provisions including sugar cane and all kinds of animals could be found. There might be chickens, pigs, goats, sheep, sometimes a young calf.

The time came for my big brother and I to look after the animals. We had to clean out the chicken coops, and the pig pens. That manure was good for the vegetable garden and other ground provisions, such as potatoes, beets, and carrots.

Back then we had no running water or electricity in our house, we had to go to the local public standpipe for water, and for light we had kerosene lamps. Our home was a one roof and a shed, two-bedroom chattel house. Most of the houses back then were made from wood in the tongue and groove style with a galvanized roof. The houses were built about three to four feet off the ground to allow for the runoff after it rains. When there was a lot of rain, our home would leak, and we would catch the water in pots and pans to keep the floor dry. The beds in our home were not at all luxurious. They were always made from crocus bags and these bags would be cut open, then bleached and washed. When they were dry, my mother would sew them together to make a big bed that is stuffed with Cuscus grass. Cuscus grass is prepared by cutting it and laying it out to dry in the sun for days. Every so often you would go and turn it over making sure that it was dry throughout because the drier the grass, the longer the bed would last.

The beds would be placed on the floor in the bedrooms, there's nothing like a new bed to sleep in for the first time. They were about two feet thick when finished, with the pillows made from the same crocus bags and stuffed with the same grass. The sheets, when they were any, were made from the same crocus bag material or my mom would credit material from the Coolie man who came through the neighborhood once a week. She made some nice flower-patterned sheets for the beds. My mom would be happy if the beds lasted two years especially with three boys sleeping in the same bed, where much bedwetting happened. I had a problem with bedwetting until I was about twelve years old. My mom tried everything that she could think of to help me. I can recall her giving me the heart of the soursop fruit saying it would help in stopping my bed wetting. I can't remember whether it worked or not. What I do remember is the problem we had with bed bugs (we call them chinks), due to the bed wetting. They used to bite the hell out of you, and they only came out at night. When the lamp was lit you could see them running for cover. When you killed them, there was so much blood that it left a stain on the sheet. Going to bed first was preferable, you didn't want to be the one in the middle of the bed. It was hell.

Four - Underneath the Cellar

The men in Buccary were typical of men of that time. Some men had two families, one family with his wife and one with the other woman. In Barbados, a man could have all the children he wanted if he was willing to support them. If the man refused to support the child which was required by law, the mother would take him to court for child support. After which he would be ordered to pay "cock-taxes" ("child support").

My dad had two families; he had eleven children that we know of, five with my mom and six with the other woman but he was married to my mom. The thing that was so interesting was, my mom and the other woman used to talk when they saw each other. My mom was a saint in my eyes and my dad was the opposite. He was busy procreating. I have a half-brother who is the same age as me, and there are two more in the family who are the same age as each other. All one can say that some years my father was very active.

It's said that "a little knowledge is a dangerous thing," and in my case this is true. I can still remember a conversation that I heard my parents were having about me. I was in trouble, so I went and hid underneath the cellar of our house waiting for my father to go to his other family. My mom said to my dad," Kenrick, you know lots of people can't you try to see if anyone can get Graydon a job, or a trade?" My father said, "Me? That blasted boy mind is as flat as his feet." When I heard him say that it hurt more than all the beatings I had ever gotten from him. Yes, I do have flat feet.

Another thing about my father's time was, that it was common to see a man beating his wife or his woman, for whatever reason and not a thing would be said or done about it. It was normal. I must say that I have never seen my dad hit my mom, but my siblings and I could tell when our parents were at odds with each other. Our mother was a devoted woman of God, she didn't talk back nor argue with our father. Instead, she would sing her favourite song for the occasion, it goes something like this: "Must Jesus bear the cross alone, and let the world go free, no, there is a cross for everyone and there's a cross for me." He would walk away from my mom, maybe because of what was said about our grandmother: People said that she used to beat up on her men. She lived next door and she could cuss better than any fisherman.

I said my mom was a saint in my eyes, but she was an earthly saint. At times she would lose her temper but sinned not. That was said to say this, one of the most vicious beatings I ever received was from my mother. Up to this day I can't recall what caused the beating. Maybe it was the straw that broke the camel's back. She beat me with anything she got her hands on at the time, at one point I was hit on my head with the heel of one of her shoes, and I lost my voice for about ten minutes. The next day the only part of my body that didn't hurt was my tongue, she had to take me to the doctor.

Five - Puberty, a Time to Remember

I discovered the birds and the bees around the age of 10. Playing show and tell and doctor was fun, until I saw the real thing for the first time. All I could think about was there was so much hair – I mean lots and lots of hair. I ran! Going through puberty wasn't easy for me. You would smell me before you saw me coming. By and by I was a walking hard-on and self-pleasuring was not only an option, but a necessity.

I thanked God for the mother I had. My mom was the type of person who would be one of the first to lend a helping hand in the neigbourhood, especially where the elderly was concerned. Because my mom was well known and respected throughout the neighbourhood, it helped save my hide on many occasions when I found myself in trouble. I wasn't considered one of the good kids in the community, however, when people in the neighborhood needed some cleanup done around their house, and errands to be run they'd call on me. I would do it for the financial benefits. I was also known for my foul mouth, and some of the young girls my age between thirteen and sixteen wouldn't keep company or have a conversation with me.

There was a family that lived in the next neighbourhood, in Lower Holders' Hill. There were plenty of kids in that family and most of them were girls; most of the kids were Brown-Skin, but the one girl named Ursula was Dark Skin. She was one of the girls who I used to interfere with, and boy did I pay for that interference! When she was in her school uniform, I couldn't take my eyes off her. The uniform was white and blue, the blouse was white; the skirt was cut high above her knees and pressed in pleats that were arranged in furrow style, looking like an accordion. When a girl is wearing a skirt such as this, she would be aware that with one wrong move the goal post would be seen. Ursula, she wasn't fat, she wasn't skinny, she wasn't ugly, she wasn't beautiful, but she was perfect.

I wasn't aware she complained to her dad about me. They lived next to Mr. Dean's rum shop, a place where I would hang out at times watching the guys playing cards and slamming dominos. One Saturday evening, I was there when her father grabbed me, and said, "My daughter is complaining that you keep bothering her." He did this in front of the crowd, and said, "I ain't going to hurt you, due to the fact you're Kenrick and Louise's child, but I'm only going to tap you." And when he tapped me with his hand, I lost my voice and plain water ran out of my mouth. I never bothered her again and whenever I saw her, I would hide or go to the other side of the road.

Six – Easter Holidays

April 1st as you know, is known for practical jokes and hoaxes. One year I fell victim in one of the fool's jokes. The Morris' second son Stephen pulled a joke on me, and it didn't end well. He called me and told me to take a note to my father, and not to open it. I gave the note to my father and when he read it, he gave me a few thumps on my head and called me a fool! Then he gave me the note to read, and it said, "Send the fool farther and farther."

As a youngster growing up in Barbados, Easter was my favourite holiday. I liked it more than Christmas. Good Friday was an interesting time for us kids in Buccary. On that day there was a family in the neighbourhood who would take an egg, break it, and separate the white from the yolk; then the egg white would be placed into a glass half full of water. It was then put in the sun before 12 O'clock. Sometime after 12 O'clock a form would appear in the glass. It could've been a boat, a plane, a coffin, or a number of other things when you looked at it. The form was supposed to tell you what the future held. I saw a plane. It said the future would turn out well for me, and it was true. That same family had a tree that bled blood when you cut into on Good Friday at 12 noon.

I used to enjoy the activities my family and others prepared for the Easter holidays. My mom would make us kids clean the house from top to bottom, inside and out. She would send us to pick some white-head bush which was prevalent at that time. It was good for scrubbing the floors, it would remove all the dirt and grime and when dry the floors would shine. On the outside, we would go around the house picking up any loose garbage and pulling weeds and bushes that were growing around the foundation. Afterwards, we would go to the beach and fetch buckets and buckets of sand to spread all around the outside making the house look really nice.

Good Friday meant we ate fish as was a tradition shared with most of the community. It didn't matter what kind it was. With so many people out looking, at times it meant that fish would be scarce. But my mom was not one to be deterred, she would go to her backup plan; the boneless Salt-Fish from Newfoundland. The meal for the day would be Rice and Peas or Coucou with Salt-Fish. To this day, I have not met anyone that can cook Coucou with Salt-Fish the way my mom used to cook it. She made it taste better than steak. It is strange how we stay with tradition; I still don't eat meat on Good Friday.

Bright and early on Saturday morning before the big day, my mother would go out in the yard to select a fowl for the big dinner. The way she chose the victim was interesting; she would catch one and put a finger up its bum to see if it was with an egg; if it was, it would be free to live another day. If not, it would be on the dinner table the next day. Easter and Christmas were the only times of the year when we kids had a choice of what kind of meat we preferred at dinner: the choices could be chicken, pork, or fish.

On Easter morning we all got up bright and early with the crowing of the cocks. By that time, my mom would have dinner halfway done. She would also have tea or cocoa with some bakes ready for us to eat before we got ready for Sunday School and Church. After Church, we would go home and have a great meal; as soon as the meal was finished, we would go to the different pastures to fly kites. I was never good at making or flying a kite, but my friend Thomas was really good at it. So, I would go with him to fly my kite. On occasion there would be a kite war; that consisted of placing a razorblade on the end of the kite's tail. With this attachment, the kites would spin and zigzag across each other.

On the Easter Monday holiday, some of us would go to Queen's Park to listen to traditional live music and see people displaying their best dresses, hats, skirts, suits, and ties in a variety of colours.

Seven – Oddest Job on Summer Vacation

Growing up on the rock (Barbados), school holidays was the thing we kids look forward to the most. Summer vacation time occurred the second week of June to the first week of September, it was the hottest time of the year, also a time of harvest. This time was meant for adventure for us kids, and for learning different things. Summer holidays also meant more chores to be done at home. Some of the older kids would be looking to do some part-time work. The job could be helping someone clean up around their home, or it could be working harvesting different crops from the fields. For the smart ones, their family would get them a job in retail or in a business office. One of the oddest jobs that I did was to help clean out a shit house (outhouse). I had befriended an older man in our neighbourhood, and he asked me if I would like a job. I said yes due to the fact the money was really good. We would go to the job site a day or two before starting the job and dig a hole about four-by-four wide, six feet deep, and about ten feet away from the old outhouse. After that, the transferring operation from the outhouse to the hole would take place at around 12 o'clock midnight. When the job was done and I got paid, my friends would see me with all that money and wanted to know where I got it from, but I wouldn't say, only Thomas knew.

Getting the chores done as soon as possible was important, the sooner it was finished, the more time we had to hangout. One of the chores we had to do was to go to different pastures and collect the dry manure from horses and cows to be used for fuel for cooking. I liked the cow manure best, when it hit the ground it would flatten out and dry smooth in the form of a frisbee. It also burned slowly and gave off good heat. The horse manure was different, it was like cricket balls sticking together, and when dry, it was lightweight and burned quickly.

With all the chores done, some of us would hangout around the local rum shops watching the men drinking Mount Gay and Cockspur rum and slamming some bones (playing dominos). That's how I learned the game. At times you would get lucky and they would let you have a game with them. Other times, we would hang out at the beach where there would be cursing, rum drinking, and gambling. There would often be two or three groups of men playing different games. The games could be three or seven card Poker, Rummy, Blackjack, or throwing bones (dice). I became a good player at some of the games. My favourites were Poker and Rummy.

Talking about gambling makes me recall an incident that happened to me one evening at home. It was about 6 o'clock, it was one of those odd times when everyone was at home. We were listening to a program coming over the Rediffusion, my mom was out in the yard making the evening snack, I can't remember whether it was tea or cocoa. Back in those days there was no such thing as breakfast, lunch, or dinner as there is today. What we call breakfast was a tin cup of tea or cocoa with biscuits, and butter spread between making them palatable to the taste. Today's lunch was our main meal of the day, and that could be a variety of different meals. They could be provisions with flying-fish, or rice and peas with Kingfish, or Coucou with salt-fish.

Excuse my getting sidetracked, let's get back to the incident I was talking about. I was at the table with my siblings waiting for our mother to come in from the yard with whatever tea or cocoa she was making for us. We had already gotten the biscuits and our father was sitting on a chair in the living room in a corner listening to the program. I was playing at the table with the biscuits pretending that I was shuffling cards getting ready to gamble. My dad saw me, and he came over and slapped me across my head so hard that he knocked me off the chair to the floor, saying that I was teaching others how to gamble. I had a ringing in my head for a few days after that.

Eight - The Good Samaritan

Back in the day growing up in the community of Paynes Bay, there were always one or two people that stood out. Miss Birch was one such person and people looked up to her. She was one of the head nurses at one of the district almshouses in the city. She was the one that people in the community sought after for advice on medical matters. I can still remember as a small child, my mother would take me to her house when I wasn't feeling well. She would give my mom something to use on me at home or give me a pill right there. My mother and others back then couldn't afford to take their children to the doctor.

Miss Birch was one of the people who would call on me to help clean up around their homes and to run errands. I enjoyed working for her because she paid well, and she would offer you food if she were cooking. Up to this day I still think of her as the lady that saved my life. There were three incidents that happened to me that are so embedded in my mind. The first one was I was in my early teens and I came down with a very bad abscessed tooth. It was so bad I was a crying baby. That's when Miss Birch came to my rescue. She took a needle that was so big you could have stitched the cow's hide with it. She took it, heating the tip of it until it was red hot, then dipped it in alcohol and stuck it into my gum. Oh! What a release that was. As a result of what she did, I'm no longer afraid of a needle being inserted in my gums.

The second time she came to my rescue, I had eaten some canned beets and got a bad case of ptomaine poisoning. My whole body was itching. She took one look at me, took me into her kitchen and made a big glass of sweet, sweet sugar water to drink, and made me stay right where I was until the itching had stopped.

Back in the day, the Coconut Creek was the famous nightclub in our area. On weekends it would have live entertainment at night. The beach side of the property where the entertainment took place was fenced off with galvanized and had a watchman. But some of us knew how to sneak in to watch the activities. One night the watchman saw us, and we ran, going through the hole in the galvanized fence. I sliced the back of my right heel badly. I wrapped it up to stop the bleeding and the first thing in the morning I was at Miss Birch's house looking for help for the third time. When she took the wrapping off, it was then I realized how severe the wound was. The first thing she did was to clean it with alcohol. Tears ran from my eyes. Then, she dug a hole in the yard about six inches deep, took some dirt from it and mixed it with aloe, dressing the wound with the mixture and then wrapped it. Within three weeks I was fully healed. Until this day, I still have the mark from the wound.

Nine - Fun in the Woods

Sandy Lane Woods was one of the places where some of us kids used to go and hang out on summer holidays. What we liked about the woods, was that it was close to our neighbourhood, and the adventures that it held for boys between ten- and fourteen-years old pretending to be Robin Hood. Imagine a group of kids without any adult supervision and all the trouble they could find themselves in. The woods were full of adventure for us. I will always remember the trees. There were the Coconut Tree, the Mile Tree, the Sack-Sack Tree, the Mahogany Tree, and many Grape Trees. Some parts of the woods had a few nice spots where one could relax and eat and occasionally, people from the country would be seen enjoying a picnic.

There were also spots of isolation and on occasion while we played, we would come across a car parked there and no one could be seen in the vehicle, yet it rocked back and forth. We couldn't have asked for better entertainment, at times we would lie low to see who emerged from the car. What can you say, kids will be kids! Another thing we liked about the woods was the way it led to the beach. When you were there you felt as though you had your own private spot. The water was turquoise green, the sand was crystal white, and Grape Trees lined the beach with their low hanging grapes that we would pick and eat in the sea.

There was a gully that ran through the woods from east to west and ended at the beach (Sandy Lane Gully). Also, a portion of Highway One used to pass through the middle of it, running from south to north. The gully was one of the spots where we used to like to hangout after a good rain, which would cause a large river to form at the end of the gully before it emptied into the Ocean. We used to like to make boats and sail them on the river. It was a sight to see the gang, including the usual suspects; Thomas, his uncle Henderson, my cousin Denzill, Winston, myself, and a few others. We would make the boats out of dry coconuts. We would take the dry coconut, split it in half and clean the inside, we would then get one or two long sticks from the coconut tree limb and some grape leaves to use as sails. The sticks were threaded through the middle of the leaves, after that they were stuck in the front part of the half coconut and there would be our boat!

Talking about boats, I just had a recollection of an incident that happened between Thomas, Denzill, and myself. We were by the same river playing and racing our boats. Suddenly, we were arguing about whose boat was the best and the fastest. Thomas and I agreed that mine was the best and fastest. Denzill didn't like that so he threw stones at my boat and sank it. Thomas said, "that's not fair." So Denzill took a stone and threw it at Thomas' boat and sunk it, and by and by there was a fight between Thomas and Denzill. Thomas won hands down. He is a friend that is closer than a brother.

We also enjoyed the Sandy Lane sugar cane factory. It was located on the east side of the woods. When in operation it was an interesting place for a visit, which we did occasionally. The tall fescue alongside the road made it a great place to hide when you were going to steal some sugar cane from the vehicles on the way to the factory. Back in that era, transportation of sugarcane to the factories was either by horse and cart or lorries. We would come out from hiding as the vehicle was passing by and take some of the cane. But there was a particular kind of cane that we went after that we really liked. It was the Brown Skin Girl. The Brown Skin Girl is a cane that is lighter in colour; softer and much larger in size with lots of juice and tastes great. The other kind was dark gray and knotty, hard to suck on and not as juicy.

Ten - Good Memories

One of the good memories that stays with me is when I was between seven and nine years old. There was the man who came around the neighbourhood pushing a two-wheel cart with blocks of ice in it, selling ice cones. He only came around on weekend afternoons, and you would hear him ringing his bell letting everyone know he was there. We kids' would come running from all around the 'hood looking to get some ice cones, one of the things that we would look forward to when playing outside in the hot weather.

The cones came in a variety of colours and flavours. Your choice of colours were red, white, blue, or yellow and the flavour options could be Strawberry, Banana, Pineapple, or Carnation Milk. Back in that time, the cost could run you between six-pence, and up to one shilling based on the size of the cone.

There were times some of us kids didn't have any money to buy a cone, so we would help the man push his cart around the neighbourhood. We would be ringing the bell, and carrying cones from house to house, hoping at the end of the day we would get some money and free ice cones to eat.

Another fond memory that I still recall was the first pair of shoes that I wore. They were made of canvas, with rubber of different colours for the soles. They were called pumps. My mom bought them from the Bata Store in the city.

It's interesting to see over time how one's memory extends. I still retain that vivid incident when I almost lost my life. This all came about because I was in the company of some well-known colourful characters in the 'hood at the time. We were going fishing, but I didn't know that it would be dynamite fishing. When the time came to dive to retrieve the fish, that's when I got into trouble. I went after a big one that started to sink, I reached it, but suddenly, I realized how deep I was and tried to reach the surface with the fish. I was in trouble, so I let go of the fish. I was losing air and didn't think I could make it back to the surface, I was so scared I soiled myself.

Another memory was when Thomas and I used to go on a Saturday theatre binge. Occasionally there were other people, but generally it was just Thomas and I. He loved the movies, so did I but I couldn't go as often as he did. He had no restrictions on him. We would start at the Bridgetown Plaza for the 9:30 morning showing, after that we would zigzag between the Empire, Globe, Olympic and the Roxy theatres. After the morning show we would move on to the midday show followed the matinee at 4:30 pm. At times we would stay in that same theatre for the 7:00 o'clock showing depending on the next feature, or we moved on to another venue. Some of the shows were double headers. When the 7:00 pm show was finished we went to the midnight showing, but we preferred to go to the Roxy for the last showing because it was a shorter walk to home from there, about 4 to 5 miles to Paynes Bay.

enjoyed a variety of movies. The classics that come to mind are, North by Northwest, West Side Story; the Pink Panther, the Great Escape and the Man Who Shot Liberty Valance. Other popular titles included the Phantom of the Opera, Psycho and Dracula. Out of all the movies we saw, Dracula was the scariest one. I had trouble sleeping for a few nights after seeing that movie.

When I'm relaxed, I remember events that now give me pause. I remember an incident that happened in our neighbourhood that's still a mystery to this day: Who poisoned the pig?

There was this man who had a big, big beautiful black and white pig. I can't recall whether it was a sow or a boar. The man was the boastful kind. He went around the 'hood saying that when he slaughtered his pig, the only niggers in the 'hood that will eat any of the pig will be his household and that he will be selling it to the hotels and guest houses. The word got out of the day for the killing. When he got up that morning, he found the pig dead. Someone had poisoned it. That was the talk of the town for weeks.

One of the scariest memories I had was when hurricane Janette hit Barbados in September 1955, I was 10 years old. Back then the weather forecast was not as accurate as it is today, but we knew that bad weather was on its way to the Island. I can recall the exact spot where I was and the time of the day when it all happened. It was about noon, and I was walking in a pathway between two cane fields. I was 300 yards from home and the silence was scary. There was a sudden burst of lightning and thunder. After that, the whole place went black. So black that I couldn't see my own hands in front of me. Soon afterwards, a deluge of rain and wind did an incredible amount of damage to the Island. In Buccary, however, we were lucky since all we had was some localized flooding.

Some of the other adorable memories I have, now that we are going down the rabbit hole, include diving for sea eggs on the shoal and eating them on the beach. I also remember hunting for sea turtles and their eggs on the beach at night (the eggs were a love potion), and if the turtles were of a certain size, we would turn them on their backs and take them to a backyard in the neighbourhood. Then, a day or two later they would be butchered.

There are some things that are so burnt into my memory that they are easy to recall. One such recollection was when I was in my mid-teens. My friends and I would go to a bar where there would be a dance floor and lots of girls to dance with. But I had a problem; I could only dance to the fast songs with no physical contact because if there was any contact in slow dancing my Tom-Pigeon always shows its head.

Another delightful memory for me is about the interesting motor vehicles back then. We had these car relics with running-boards and indicators coming out of their sides, and to start them you had to manually crank them. The popular models we're talking about were the Austin and Morris cars.

Eleven - Dark memories

When I look back at my childhood, the ages between ten and fourteen years were some of the darkest memories for me. I remember a time I stole six-pence (six cents) from my dad, to pay a man for some Potato slips to feed the animals. Most evenings my dad and mom would be in the backyard sitting and talking about whatever. My mother usually had something on the fire going. This evening in particular my father was there in the backyard, and my mother had a pot of boiling water on the fire. To this day I don't know how he found out that it was me who stole the money. I walked past him that evening and he grabbed me and pushed both of my hands into the boiling water on the fire and said, "that's what you get when you are a thief."

That incident took me to a dark, dark, dark period in my young life. My brother Warren used to get his share of beatings from our dad; but I was the one that got most of the whopping. I tried to talk Warren into poisoning our dad, and he said "no" and that was that. Nothing was ever said about it until our parents had passed away. He told two of my other siblings about it, and they asked if it was true. I said "yes" and their faces said it all. That period of my life was so bad, I gave some serious thoughts about ending it all. One day I was so distraught I found myself by a deserted well thinking why not just jump in, no more worries. But thank God I made a different choice right then and there.

It is still a sad moment for me when I think about all the things that I learned when I was under the cellar of our house, fighting a dog for a good position so that I could hear what my parents were talking about. As a result of some of the things I heard, when I was between 13 & 14, I ended up in Jenkins (the mad house), today it's called the mental hospital. I was there because my parents couldn't put up with my bad behaviour anymore. I used to swear plenty, and at times I would have fights with other kids in the 'hood and their parents would complain about me. I would also stay away from home for days. My parents thought one day I might end up dead, so my mom took me to see the doctor and he recommended the hospital. To this day I can still recall the cell that I was locked up in. I was thirteen going fourteen, maybe due to my age that I was not put in the public area in the hospital. The cells at Jenkins were about 8ft long, 5ft wide, and 9ft high made from soft stones and cement finish. The door was made of metal, and the top half of the door had bars about three to four inches apart so that the orderly could see into the cell. The bed frame was also made of metal, with some padding on top for the bed. The light switch for the room was on the outside of the wall, so you had no control over when it would be on or off. By 6pm you would be locked up. There were no facilities in the room, so when the time came you used what was under the bed, which was a pail that you emptied in the morning.

I was there for almost a month and was an outside patient for a while. The roughest time for me was the Electric Treatment. They would come and take you to this room that looked like an operating room in a hospital. The first time I received the treatment they were so nice to me I thought I was special, until they took me into that room, strapped me down, put that thing in my mouth, and zapped me. The next thing I know I'm in my room waking up. I remember one of the funniest things that happened when I was there. My father would have killed me if he ever saw me smoking, and here I was in this mad house getting an allotment of three cigarettes a day. I remember the brand name of those cigarettes. They were Three-Plys. The first one I got was after my first treatment, and I was in la-la land after I smoked it. These cigarettes were quite strong. Time and grandchildren doesn't allow me to say more.

My mother and one other person from the community were the only two people who came to visit me when I was in the asylum. When I came home some people in the community were nice, and others not so nice. They would call me all kinds of names, but I got over that soon. Even some of my friends had fun at my peace of mind. However, friends at that age didn't know any better, so I didn't take it personally.

Here I am in my seventies, and I still cannot bring myself to say that I ever had love for my father. I did know that I hated him and was afraid of him. He and I never had a real conversation until I was in my forties and that was a result of me being able to leave the island in my late teens. The one thing that I still cannot get over was how quiet a man he was, out of all the men in Buccary, he was the quietest. He was also the cruelest S.O.B. for a father! But when all is said and done, I took some good from it all. There were times when I found myself in situations and the thought that he would find out was enough to stop me. I also think that I am a good father, because I make sure that I am the opposite of him.

Twelve – Politics and the Ordinary Man

In the early 60s I started to pay attention to Barbados politics. I was in my middle teens. Back in that time, politics was to a great degree dogmatic and funny at the same time. Back then there was no television and few people had radios for the politicians to use to get their message across. So, what they would do was find someone in the neighbourhood of the same political stripe, and that person would be the mouthpiece for Mr. Politician. I call him Mr. because it was a man's world where politics was concerned, and women were considered homemakers.

The good thing about politics in Barbados in that, it is civil and democratic. The political season came around at least every five years. During that time, some people would follow the politicians from neighbourhood to neighbourhood. The fun part of politics for me was when the politicians visited the local rum shops. In my part of the 'hood, we had Mr. Low's, Mr. Deans', and Early Brathwaite rum shops. The most famous shop was Mr. Low's. Some of us called him Aunty Low in our conversations, but never to his face. His shop was located on Highway One in Paynes Bay, St. James. It was a major stomping ground for the locals and others passing through. He was a well-respected member of the community. I would go from shop to shop and listen to all the B.S., but my true purpose was getting all the free food and drinks you could have. If the politician thought you were going to vote for him, then the sky was the limit. The good thing about all this political stuff, was that you would get to do it all over again when his opponent came looking for your vote.

In that era politicians could be entertaining. I saw things that a politician did and heard things he would do if he were elected that made me say "Wow!" Did he mean what he said? I remember a time when a group of us were on the beach gambling, and this politician came and started canvassing the crowd. By and by he was gambling and losing on purpose. It was plain he was trying to buy our votes. One of the best memories for me of a politician doing his stuff, was in Buccary. It was in our backyard and my mom and a few women were talking and eating, when this politician walked right into the yard to join the women in conversation. He asked if he could have some of what they were eating and drinking. The utensils at our house were not luxurious: the cups, plates, bowls, spoons, and forks were made of tin and the pots were made of cast iron. He met them where the rubber meets the road and won some votes, including my mother's.

In that era, the peoples' consensus of the parties was that the Barbados Labour Party (B.L.P.) was thought of as being in favour of business and plantation owners, while the Democratic Labour Party (D.L.P.) was seen as looking out for the working class. And then there was Mr. Ernest Mottley, the City Mayor who was thought of as the poor man's politician.

 I remember when the Democratic Labour Party won the national election in 1961. With the excellent Errol Barrow as the leader, and the slogan of the time was "We swept them out" meaning the opposition, the Barbados Labour Party. Oh! What a celebration that was, people were dancing in the streets, the rum shops filled with patrons drinking and partying. On Highway One that passes through Paynes Bay, there was a large parade of vehicles with horns blasting and flags flying, and people with brooms mimicking the sweeping out of the opposition.

Thirteen - Spark Plug

The Morris family stood out in our community. They had the biggest house and the nicest of things in Buccary. Their kids would have all kinds of toys to play with, so some of us would hang out and play with them. Back in that time, the Morris' had the only good radio in the community. The reason the reception was very good there was because of a big, tall Mile-Tree that grew beside their house. Their oldest son Cecil, would make an antenna, take it up the tree as far as possible, then connect it to the radio. Because of that he was able to receive reception from all over the world. People would come from around the community, to listen to the different kinds of programs. We were able to listen to Cricket from England, when the West Indies was playing them, also Boxing from the USA, and news from around the World.

Mr. Morris was a good father; he was one of the dads that would be seen playing games with the kids: playing Cricket, flying kites, and playing dominoes. He was also one of the men with two families. There were times back in then that I wished he was my dad. He worked at the sugar cane factory, Sandy Lane, and his job was driving a truck carrying sugar from the factory to the harbour. He was also a jack-of-all-trades at the factory. When I was around fifteen years old, he helped me to get a part time job at the factory. After the crop season was finished, they would get people to come in and clean the place and get it ready for the coming season. One of the jobs I had was to clean out a big vat. You would have to climb down a ladder into it, with a pick, shovel, hammer, and chisel to clean it out.

As a result of that job, I have a nickname which I'm still called to this day. There were two gentlemen from England in charge of the operation of the factory, both of which were colourful characters. Mr. Jack Thorne, and Mr. McGee were their names. Neither of them stood for any B.S. from the employees. Jack Thorne was the manager and a mean one. He was a modern-day slave master. Most of the men at the factory were afraid of him being as he could cuss better than they could. He was the kind of guy who considers himself a man of stature. Whenever you saw him, he would be dressed in short pants, Khaki uniform, with long turquoise socks up to the knees and brown leather boots. But McGee was the opposite of him in all aspects. He was short in stature, he was liked by the men, and you could have a conversation with him. I was one of those kids who wouldn't keep his mouth shut and always had to say something. At times, McGee would come around to see how the job was progressing, and there was a time when some of us were in a group talking, and he came and wanted to know what's wrong. I was the first to open my mouth, and when I was finished. He said, "I was like a Spark Plug, my mouth is always going." And that nickname stuck to me.

They closed the factory about a year and half after I worked there, and that was a big change for our community. Everyone was worrying and talking about all the men that would be out of work, and how they would be able to feed their families. Everything turned out to be a blessing in the end for our community. The factory was demolished, and a golf course took its place. The main road was shifted to make room for a luxury hotel and anyone who wanted a job could get one in varying degrees. As mentioned before, Mr. Jack Throne oversaw the men building the golf course, and Mr. Morris and some other men from the factory were in the crew. Thanks to that golf course, my life was changed.

Fourteen - My Introduction to Golf

There was an event that changed my life and by extension, my family also. The year was 1961, and a man we knew, Mr. Austin Griffith, came into Buccary and asked me if I would like a job working as a caddy. I didn't have the faintest clue what he was talking about caddying, but once he explained it, I was all in. The hotel was finished, and the nine-hole golf course was near completion, but the driving range was already open. The job was picking up balls on the range and taking them back to the man so he could hit them again. The job had a little bit of danger to it, because when you were out on the range about 200 to 250 yards, and the balls were being hit in your vicinity, one had to be careful not to get hit. I loved the job because the money was good, and if you were fortunate to get four or five jobs in a day you were a happy lad.

The pay was a dollar an hour, but most of the time you would get a U.S. or Canadian dollar, and sometimes a British Pound. Most of the people would give more than the dollar, and I would ask when they would be back. I started to live a life that I used to dream about, but more about that later. The best time to get a job was between 7am to 11am or 2pm to 6pm as people avoid the hottest part of the day. That was when some of us caddies would go into the woods, and do a little gambling, cooking, and drinking by the gully. One time we were down there, and all at a sudden Jack Thorne appeared out of thin air and kicked the food off the fire and sent us scattering.

The course officially opened in 1962 as a nine-hole golf course (Sandy Lane). At the time there was only one other course on the island which was Rockley Golf Club. Rockley has been in operation since the '40s and was also a nine-hole course. As local kids picking up balls on the range, we didn't have a clue how to be a real caddy. Austin Griffith got me the caddy job. He had been a caddy at Rockley back in the day, and now when everything was ready for the Sandy Lane opening, we found out Mr. Thorne would oversee the whole operation, Austin would be in charge of the golf shop and would also be the Caddy Master. As the Caddy Master, he cleverly brought about a dozen caddies from Rockley to show us how to do the job. For the first few weeks he would make sure that when the local caddies were going out on the course there would be one caddy from Rockley in the group.

I thought that picking up balls was good money, but not in comparison to caddying, when you would get four to five dollars for carrying a bag nine holes. When being a caddy, you got to meet some interesting people. I met the Beatles before they were famous. They were staying in a house by the ninth green. When the word got out that there was money in caddying, young guys from other neighbourhoods came looking for jobs as well, even the gang I ran with, including Thomas, his uncle, Henderson, my cousin Denzill, Winston and others. They all started caddying. Oh! What a change that took place in our lives! We were barefoot when we started caddying, and within a couple of months some of us were unrecognizable. We went from rags to riches.

One year after the course was open it was booming with activity. Sandy Lane became very popular. It was new, it was a bigger course than Rockley, and it was where most of the tourists went to play when on the island. So, because Rockley wasn't as busy, more caddies moved from Rockley to Sandy Lane. This resulted in less work for me. There was a time when I would carry two bags at the same time for nine holes. But now I would have to wait my turn for a job. Instead of caddying for 2 people at a time, now there would be a caddy for each golfer.

Fifteen - Education and Philosophy

Some of the best education and philosophy in my life I learnt from being a caddy. As time moved on, I developed some friendships with some of the caddies from Rockley. From them I got to learn the tricks of the trade and some of those tricks were not my finest hour. Some people would remember what type and how many golf balls they had in their bags. One thing that was a no-no; you were not to do any tricks on guests that would be staying for a week or more. When you got a new job, the first thing you would do was to find out how long they will be staying, because if they were staying for more than a couple of weeks you would do your best, so that when they returned, they would ask for you. Having guests to caddy for, for that length of time was good steady pay, and when they were leaving a bonus was often offered.

September to April was the best time for caddying. I made some good money. I was able to help out at home by giving my mom money every week to help buy food and stuff for my siblings. Back then I was making more money than my dad, and if he knew that I gave my mom any money for the week he would withhold some of what he usually gave her for running the home that week. So, I made sure that when I gave my mom any money, he wouldn't find out about it, and if there was something in particular she needed I would go and buy it for her. I am the one who brought electricity and water to our home.

As a young man and having all that money available to me, some bad habits crept into my life, and one of them was gambling. When you went down in the gully on Friday and Saturday evenings you would think it was a casino. After the gully, you go home and change clothes, and then downtown we go to Bridgetown! The introduction to the night life was a whole new world to both Thomas and I. There were two places famous for the night life, Church Village and Nelson Street and we were like kids in a candy store when we visited those places. They were so distinct from each other: Church Village was the poor man's location, with plenty of chattel houses with narrow laneways, and kerosene lamps for lights. Nelson Street was our Paris, with buildings two and three stories high on both sides of the street. There was electricity for lights, rum shops with jukeboxes playing all kinds of music, and at times you would get live entertainment. Back then the oldest profession was not condemned nor condoned but was tolerated.

There are stories that some of us still talk about of bygone days we had in Church Village and Nelson Street. A story was told about one of our friends who was a caddy. It was about the first time he had sex with a real woman, it was in the Village; it was said that when he reached the grand finale, he shouted out: "I feel like a sugar cake!" Sugar cakes are very, very sweet so that became his nickname for a while. Another story I was privy to was when a group of us were in the Village on a Saturday night, and lo and behold one of the guys' fathers was coming down the far end of the lane way. We had to run and hide.

Sixteen - Sandy Lane Caddies Strike

Before we realized it caddying became very political, and Austin the Caddy Master was the culprit. He started showing favour to the Rockley caddies that caused some ill will among us. Then he made matters worse by making one of them the Head Caddy. The Head Caddy had the power to choose when and who got a job. Thanks to their positions they knew the best paying customers from the big hotels; therefore, some of us local caddies were at their mercy to get one of those good paying jobs. During the golf season, the course got so busy that the hotels and the cruise ships operators had to make reservations for their guests.

The whole caddy business evolved, and it wasn't for the better, it became very upscale: the golf shop and the clubhouse were renovated. They also built a new members' lounge and a caddy shack. The demarcation line now came into play. Previously, we were free to go anywhere on the property and dress the way we pleased and now all of that came to a sudden end. We now had a dress code and had to stay in the caddy shack until your name was called. So, a new kind of game came into play. Since most of the people who came to play would be staying for a week or more, now when you got a job, you didn't let anyone know how long the guest would be staying, or how well they paid because you could lose the job to one of the chosen. Most of the golfing guests were staying at the Sandy Lane luxury hotel and to this day Sandy Lane is still-the most luxurious and expensive hotel on the Island. Any guest from the hotel was given special treatment. There were other luxury hotels in the area which were good for business as well, such as the Coral Reef Club, and the Colony Club.

Between the caddying politics and the demarcation line, we were able to find out some things that were happening. One of them was the kickback scheme. The way it was told to me by one of the guys, you had to pay. Austin the caddy master, and David the head caddy, were both heavy smokers and drinkers. So, keeping them supplied with smokes and drinks was to your benefit. As time moved on, conditions were not improving. We couldn't get even a glass of cold water or purchase a drink from the club house. And to make matters worse, someone in management decided that the basic caddy pay should be cut to $1.50 from $2.00. We had had enough and couldn't take anymore. We went on strike. The strike was not long, and we didn't lose any pay, but I was labeled a troublemaker. I was called a troublemaker because a reporter from the Advocate Newspaper Interview some of us, and I was the one that he quoted in the papers.

At the golf course most caddies had nicknames that were colourful, such as Pinky, Blackie, Darky, Poor Boy, Sandfly, Tom Cat, and Yellowman. My friend Thomas' nickname was Bush, and our other friend nickname was Lad Mouse. Then there was me, Spark Plug. The newspaper had big front-page news, Sandy Lane caddies went on strike, and Spark Plug said, "conditions must get better and the caddy's pay returned to where it was before. If not, his sparks were going to fly, and they weren't going to like it." The powers to be didn't like what was said and I was punished, by not being able to caddy for a week. Some said that I had to learn how to keep my mouth shut.
But I was famous for a week or two, Spark Plug said this! Spark Plug said that! So, the name in various degrees stuck with me for life, but not I'm not offended by it.

When I returned after the week, feelings were still a little raw where some people were concerned. I was in the caddy shack for a few days before I got a job. The only reason that I got that job was because there was no one else available. Things did get a little easier, I learned how to play the game of life. However, the owner of the business, Mr. Ronald Trees, an

Englishman who loved the game but was lousy at it, had his own personal caddy. Whenever he came to play there would be other people with him, and most caddies didn't want to be in that group. He was cheaper than dirt, and he would insist that he pay for the caddies. To make things worse the caddy master was the one who came out to pay you on his behalf so there would be no tip or extras of any kind.

Seventeen - Mr. Caulkins: A Blessing from God

One Saturday evening about 3.30pm, Mr. Trees and three others came to play. There were a good number of caddies in the shack at the time and there was an un-written rule: if you refused a job chances were you wouldn't get another job for the rest of the day. On this day, when they came out to choose the caddies for the group, I was one of the first to be picked. And I knew the reason why, but as fate would have it, it turned out to be a blessing for me. The job I got that evening was a gentleman named Mr. Dan P. Caulkins who was an American. His wife was also in the group so her caddy and I had a little talk about how we should caddy for them. At times you would only be a bag carrier because you knew the end results. So, we decided to do our stuff. We made sure that no one lost a ball, and the clubs were always clean. And we kept them engaged in conversation about the course and the island, because this was their first time in Barbados.

At the end of the round, Mr. Caulkins gave me two U.S. dollars as a tip and asked if I would be available for the next day that he and his wife would play at the same time. I said, "yes, I will be waiting for you sir." As expected, the caddy master came out and paid us. I didn't say anything about the good tip and that they were playing the next day. I went to the club the next day and got a morning job and left at noon. The reason I left was because if I got another job that would mean I wouldn't be able to caddy for him at 3.30pm. So, I went into the gully and hung out for a while, then about 2:45pm I went back to the shack and waited. He was right on time, and he asked if Spark Plug was around. It was the beginning of a friendship that lasted a lifetime.

The way things turned out it was as though Mr. Caulkins was a blessing sent from God for me. It turned out that he was staying in one of the new beach houses by the woods which was within walking distance to the club. As fate would have it, my first cousin was the head maid at his beach house. He said he would be staying for three weeks and would like me to caddy for him for the time. Sometimes he would come by himself to play and let me play a few holes with him, and he and I talked about all kinds of things. I also told him that his head maid was my cousin, and we had a good laugh about that. I didn't think he believed at the time, since he did ask her if it was so. After the third time caddying for him, he said to me "Sparky, I will pay you weekly for caddying for me." I said, "yes sir." All of which turned out in my favour. Whether he played or not, he still paid me. At times he would let me know ahead of time that he wouldn't be playing the next day. Most of those times I was able to get a job for the evening. The powers to be started to notice how well I was being treated by him and asked me lots of questions. At times he would bring guests with him and some caddies tried their best to be in the group as they knew that it would be a good job.

Mr. Caulkins was a very generous man. The first week he paid me for caddying, I couldn't believe my eyes. He gave me $25 US dollars, which was lots and lots of money back then. And for the next two weeks I made sure that I wouldn't miss one day caddying for him. If I waited for him at the club and something came up that he couldn't make it, he would call the club to tell me he couldn't make it. Even the caddy master was impressed by the call. There were moments which you were not sure about, but you knew that a paradigm shift had taken place. Mr. Caulkins was a personal friend of the owner of the club, and he is calling me to say that he wouldn't be there, and to make things even better at times he would give me a ride home. We went in the same direction for home. After all of that, my status was elevated, and I could do no wrong.

When the time was near for him to leave, he invited me for a drink at his place, along with his wife and my cousin and we had a good time. The day before he was leaving, he and his wife came to play, and let her caddy and I play with them. At the end of the round, he said," Sparky, I would like to keep in touch with you, I will be coming back every year." I said, "yes sir." He said, "Mr. Caulkins would do." We exchanged addresses. I made sure that the clubs were all nice and clean and ready for travel. We said our goodbyes and he gave me an envelope, and when he was gone I opened it and there was $50 U.S. in it. I was speechless when I saw the $50! So much so that the only person I told about it was Thomas. The next day I went downtown and bought myself a nice shirt and a pair of pants.

Eighteen - The Change

Mr. Caulkins was a man of his word. He did keep in touch with me and sent a nice Christmas gift for me. He also told me that he would be back either October or November next year but will send me a definite time when he is sure. In the meantime, the course at Sandy Lane was in full swing. One evening the owner came to play and as usual he had company, and low and behold one of them asked if Spark Plug was available. It turned out that he was a friend of Mr. Caulkins, and that he was told to ask for me when he got to the club. On a few other occasions, some more of his friends would come looking for me to caddy for them. He was sure looking out for me even though he wasn't on the Island. Whenever I caddied for one of his friends, I would drop him a line to say thanks.

As the season was slowing down at the end of April, I wrote and told him that I wouldn't be going to the course as often, but I would be working in my kitchen garden until things started up again. Come September I would be back at the club every day. Sometimes, it seems there are things you cannot explain, and you just go with it. After I told him what my plans were for the summer, every month I got funds from him. That same summer a change took place in my life. The Payne's Bay Pentecostal church that I used to go to as a kid for Sunday school and church service with my mom, had an evangelistic revival service going on for a week. When the church held such services there would be large gatherings around the church and my friends and I hung around because of all the nice young ladies that would be there. I don't know what quite happened to me, but about the fourth night I found myself at the altar confessing my sins and asking God for forgiveness.

So, because of that, I was the topic of the community for a while. Some people didn't believe it. Some made fun of me and said I was out of my mind, and some encouraged me to keep it up, my mom being one of them. The change that took place in my life was instant: I stopped cursing, I stopped drinking, I stopped gambling, and I stopped going to the nightclubs and other things. I just didn't do them anymore. Some of my friends would try to get me into the old habits but I would always decline. That same year in September, I was baptized on a Sunday morning in the sea at Paynes Bay, and lots of people were there to see for themselves if Spark Plug was really going to be baptized.

When I went back to caddying, the guys had their fun calling me all kinds of names and reminded me not to use any more tricks of the trade. Mr. Caulkins was back in November and we carried on as usual. He even brought me some of his old clubs from home. I told him about the change that took place in my life, and he said, "that's good for you Sparky."
Sometimes we would have a talk about God and the church stuff, not sure he was into it. However, when I caddied for him on Sunday evening, he would always ask how the service was. Now that he knows where I live, he would often give me a ride home. One day he asked me what kind of transportation I would like to go back and forth to the club. That same evening, I introduced him to my mom and my siblings and showed him my kitchen garden.

The next day he commented on my family and the kitchen garden. He noted that the family seemed nice, and the garden was in good shape. Then, he said, "you still haven't answered my question about transportation issues," I said, "Mr. Caulkins, what I would really like is to have my own house." He said nothing after I said that, and we kept playing. There was another day we were on the course and an airplane passed low over the golf course, and I said in jest, "I wonder what it feels like to be in an airplane." I didn't realize that he was paying close attention to the things that I was saying. Two days before he was to leave, he said, "Sparky, how much would it cost for a house you are thinking about?" I told him what I thought it would cost and how I would go about getting it. "Sounds like a good plan," he said.

The last day as usual before he left, we had a game to see who the better golfer was. He had been the better golfer when we first played, not anymore. When we finished, he said, "Sparky, your game has improved." He took me to one side and said, "Here's some funds to help you get started on the house." The next day I went to Speightstown to the building supply company, Plantation Limited, to inquire how much material was needed and what would be the cost for the house I had in mind. Credit was established and within six weeks I had a house on the spot where my Kitchen Garden used to be. With the necessary upkeep through the years the house is still standing.

Nineteen - The Feel

In January 1964, I got a letter from Mr. Caulkins asking me if I would like to come for a visit and work on his beef farm and I enthusiastically said "yes." It was April before all the necessary travel documents were completed. Suddenly, I was amazed at the place I found myself. At Seawell International Airport, sitting in a DC-7, four engine propeller aircraft on my way to New York, New York. I would get to know what it felt like to be in an airplane. As I sat on the plane, I thought about how I was thought to be the black sheep of the family and was looked down on by some people of the community. Only God in his infinite mercy could pull off something like this. There I was on my way to New York City to start a new chapter in my life.

Epilogue

Writing this collection of memories was a bittersweet experience for me. When I think about where I started from and how far I've come, I am grateful. I consider myself lucky to have been able to choose a path through what some might consider disadvantage, to a life of peace and contentment.

I will admit, the most bitter and damaging part of my life was my relationship with my father. From what I recall, he never once said anything nice to me or about me. It was something I felt well into my forties when I was able to release my resentment and see him as he was.

Thank God for our mother, who was always there to show us she had faith in us and loved us deeply. She was the rock of our family and was always ready to help when we needed it. One thing I learned, and something I've benefited from is the knowledge that one person can make a difference in your life and for me that person was Mr. Caulkins. From the moment I met him my life and the life of my family changed for the better and he is the reason I'm living in North America today.

There is a quote that has stuck with me although I don't know who said it, and it goes like this: "Make peace with your past so it doesn't screw with your present." I've used this as a guide throughout my life and today I live in Canada with my beautiful wife, two amazing children I am incredibly proud of, and three awesome grandkids - the light of my life. I am blessed to be able to enjoy a comfortable home and to enjoy my retirement that includes playing lots of golf...my passion since earlier days.

Made in the USA
Monee, IL
09 May 2021